PRACTICE MAKES PERFECT

Further classroom titles from LinguaBooks

Academic Presenting and Presentations
A preparation course for university students
978-1911369240

In A Strange Land
Short stories for creative learning
978-1911369189

A Busker on Bow Street
Short stories for adult learners No. 1
978-1911369103

Lost Dreams
Short stories for adult learners No. 2
978-1911369110

The Farmer's Son
Short stories for adult learners No. 3
978-1911369127

The Seasonal Visitor
Short stories for adult learners No. 4
978-1911369134

PRACTICE MAKES PERFECT

Partner Grammar Drills
for English Language Learners

CEFR Level B2
Upper Intermediate

Andrew Garth

Copyright © 2020 LinguaBooks

A CIP catalogue record for this publication is available
from the British Library.

ISBN: 978-1-911369-52-3

Editor: Ann Claypole
Proofreader: Marie-Christin Strobel

Cover design: Maurice Claypole

Images: ID 108603977 © Kadettmann, ID 114538077 © Pleprakaymas, ID 103982191 © Makidotvn, ID 18035775 © Monkey Business Images, ID 30881557 © Wavebreakmedia Ltd | Dreamstime.com

LinguaBooks
Elsie Whiteley Innovation Centre
Hopwood Lane, Halifax HX1 5ER
United Kingdom

www.linguabooks.com

I am not afraid of storms for I am learning how to sail my ship

Louisa May Alcott

Author's Note

This book represents a compilation of grammar lessons based on a practical method I have developed during the course of my teaching career. The lessons have been honed over many hours of classroom testing and revision, resulting in a product I am proud to share.

I hope this book helps your students as much as it has helped mine.

TABLE OF CONTENTS

Introduction

This book was written to solve a problem commonly encountered in the teaching of English as a foreign or second language, whereby students are able to master key grammatical aspects of the English language when writing but fail to achieve sufficient accuracy when speaking. With certain grammatical points in particular, merely correcting and explaining these specific grammatical errors often yields minimal results. The method used in this book is based on the author's practical experience and proven success.

At the heart of this method is quasi-repetitive, targeted spoken practice reinforced by immediate and accurate feedback. Unlike conventional drills based solely on the audio-lingual approach, the student activities presented here offer dynamic variants which draw on the fractal approach to language teaching in that they present self-similar patterns of language use rather than the enforced repetition of linguistic microstructures.

Whereas behaviourist drills typically rely on a spoken model provided by the teacher, *Practice Makes Perfect* harnesses student-to-student interaction so that both stimulus and response contribute to the learning effect. Furthermore, the flexible pace of pair work embraces additional scope for reflection and endorsement, and for this reason Q&A and substitution techniques take precedence over mere repetition drills.

These activities are truly innovative in that they combine the spontaneity of traditional drills with a cognitive focus designed to enhance understanding through a holistic process of reading, speaking, responding, correcting and assimilating with the ultimate goal of enhancing accuracy and improving retention.

Since the success of any classroom activity depends on maintaining interest and alertness, these drills have also been designed to be entertaining; their effectiveness is all the greater because they are fun to use.

Since the students work in pairs, alternately quizzing and correcting one another, there is a constant change of activity and focus. Each drill item lasts just a moment and the concept works equally well regardless of class size. In the case of large classes in particular, the amount of immediate feedback that teachers can give is strictly limited, but this method allows the students to provide instant and accurate feedback to one another. Experience has shown that not only do learners enjoy the quizzing nature of the drills, but also their grammatical accuracy improves quickly.

Although the methodology is communicative in nature, its use is not limited to the conventions of conversational Englsh. Grammatical structures which are more common in written than in spoken English (for example, it-cleft sentences; see Unit 9) can also be practised and reinforced through spoken drills and partner practice, adding greater immediacy and a keener sense of usage than can be achieved through written practice.

This book serves a dual purpose. It incorporates a set of ready-made interactive components which can be used within the context of any type of lesson, whether communicative, task-based or using any other overall methodology, and it also provides a conceptual framework for teachers to adapt the technique to suit their own student base and teaching context, for example in the fields of Content and Language Integrated Learning, English for Specific Purposes or English for Academic Purposes or any other specialised area of English Language Teaching.

For this reason, the selection of grammatical items is an empirical rather than an exhaustive one; it lays no claim to completeness but represents a selection of lessons which have proven to be effective in practice and fun to use. Furthermore, it provides the language teacher with a new framework for independent experimentation, development and extension.

How to use this book

Each unit consists of three parts – a grammar presentation, a corresponding set of grammar drills (partner practice) and a number of additional speaking activities. The focus throughout is on pair work and to this end, each Core Unit in Part One begins with a sequence of illustrative dialogues followed by a brief explanation and further examples of the target structures in use. Unit headings are communicative and intuitive (e.g. 'What time did you get up?') in order to minimise the use of grammatical metalanguage at the outset. A cognitive learning phase is provided by means of a condensed introduction to each key grammar point. In a classroom situation, the teacher is free to elaborate on the formal grammar introduction in each respective Core Unit or to proceed swiftly to the grammar drills and speaking activities. The grammar drills are found in Part Two and Part Three and take the form of guided mini-dialogues whereby students work in pairs and correct each others' responses. This unique approach enables the technique to be used independently of direct teacher intervention and is therefore suitable for a wide variety of learning situations, including very large classes where it is often very difficult to combine holistic speaking practice with effective progress in microlearning.

Following the guided pair work, the students return to the Core Unit for further speaking practice and reinforcement. Each unit is therefore constructed as a self-contained lesson, but the individual components can also be used selectively to support conventional teaching methods and course materials.

PART ONE
Core Units

UNIT 1
'What time did you get up?'

Hi Paula, how are you today?

I'm very tired. I got up at four o'clock this morning.

What time did you get up?

Four o'clock. I had to catch an early train.

I know how you feel. It took me five hours to get here.

What? How long did it take you?

Five hours. I came by bus.

Responding with open questions

Open questions can be used to show that certain information is surprising or to express interest. These questions begin with a question word such as **who**, **what**, **when**, **where**, **which** or **how**. The same question forms can be used to indicate that information was not fully understood.

In order to express surprise or seek confirmation in spoken English, the question word is <u>stressed</u> with rising intonation (↗) and the question ends with falling intonation (↘).

I read three English novels every week.

↗<u>How many</u> English novels do you read every week?↘

I used to work for Bill Gates.

I lived in Siberia when I was at university.

↗<u>Who</u> did you use to work for?↘

↗<u>Where</u> did you live when you were at university?↘

I've been to 135 countries.

↗<u>How many</u> countries have you been to?↘

SPEAKING ACTIVITIES 1

1 Grammar Drills

Practice with a partner. **Student A**, go to page 36. **Student B**, go to page 58.

2 A crazy weekend

It is Monday morning. You had a very unusual weekend. So did your partner. Tell each other what you did. Express surprise and ask them to confirm what they have said or to ask for more information. Use the list below or invent other situations.

Example

I flew to Paris. -> Where did you fly to?

I flew to Paris.	I had five dates.	I went skydiving.
I worked for 12 hours straight.	I drove a Ferrari.	I saved someone's life.
I found 1,000 dollars in the street.	I watched 10 movies.	I received a 100-dollar tip.
I met Brad Pitt.	I sang a song with Bob Dylan.	I swam 50 miles.

3 An unusual career

Read the passage below and take turns to ask each other questions to confirm the information given.

Example

Where was he born? -> He was born in the Kingdom of Württemberg.

He was born in the Kingdom of Württemberg in 1879 but a year later his family moved to the city of Munich in Bavaria where his father was the co-founder of an electrical equipment company.

He started school at the age of five, attending a Catholic elementary school in Munich. In 1894 the family moved to Italy, first to Milan, then to Pavia. His favourite philosopher was Immanuel Kant, whose *Critique of Pure Reason* he read at the age of 13. He studied for a teaching diploma in mathematics and physics at Zurich Polytechnic but had difficulty in finding a teaching post. Eventually, he managed to get a job at the patent office in Berne. Whilst working at this job, he wrote a number of scientific papers and received a PhD from the University of Zurich in April 1905. Later in life, he moved to the United States and became an American citizen in 1940.

He supported many causes, becoming a member of the National Association for the Advancement of Colored People and helping to establish the Hebrew University of Jerusalem. In 1952 he turned down an offer to become President of Israel.

Although he was interested in many things, one of his greatest loves was music and he was a passionate violin player.

When he died in 1955, he was one of the most famous and respected scientists in the world.

4 Who was he?

Discuss who you think the person the passage above is and say which facts give you clues to his identity.

UNIT 2
'So do I.'

I go swimming every morning.

So do I. I go to the public pool.

I don't. We have our own pool.

Sounds great! But I'm not a very good swimmer anyway.

Neither am I, but I need the exercise.

I don't. I just enjoy being in the water.

Auxiliary verbs after *so* and *neither*

We use **so** and **neither** followed by an auxiliary verb in order to avoid repetition in a follow-up sentence. In this structure, the subject of the follow-up sentence refers to a different person, e.g. 'Hassan's a teacher.' 'So is Karl.' (= 'Karl is a teacher, too.')

The auxiliary verb of the follow-up sentence has the same tense as the main verb in the original sentence. Subject and verb are inverted.

An affirmative follow-up sentence begins with **So**: 'Caitlin likes sports.' 'So do I.' (= 'I also like sports.') A negative follow-up sentence begins with **Neither**: 'Lucia doesn't like dogs.' 'Neither do I.' (= 'I don't like dogs either.')

Sometimes we use an auxiliary verb to express the opposite of a previous statement. In this case, we do not invert subject and verb: 'I haven't been to Thailand.' – 'I have.'; 'I can ride a motorbike.' – 'I can't.'

I play the guitar.

So do I.

I always hand my work in on time.

I don't.

My brother doesn't play football.

Mine does. He's in the college team.

I didn't go shopping yesterday.

Neither did I.

I'm hungry.

So am I.

I wasn't born in Europe.

I was.

SPEAKING ACTIVITIES 2

1 Grammar Drills
Practice with a partner. **Student A**, go to page 38. **Student B**, go to page 60.

2 A race to five
Look at the list of statements below. Pick one statement and read it to your partner. If they respond correctly using an auxiliary verb, they receive one point. Then they will read a sentence for you. If you respond correctly using an auxiliary verb, you receive one point. Take turns. The first person with five points wins.

Example
I live in a city -> So do I/I don't. / I don't like seafood. -> Neither do I/I do.

I live in a city.   *I don't like seafood.*   I have a younger brother.

I don't usually wake up before 8 am.   I always make my bed before I leave the house.

I would like a cup of coffee right now.   I'm good at languages.

I live in an apartment.   I have never travelled to another country.

I can drive a car.   I know how to play piano. I went to the gym today.

I received good grades in elementary school.   I can whistle.   I was born in the winter.

I can't swim.   I am not smart.   I won't receive an A in English class.

I have flown in a helicopter.   I don't always do my homework.

3 Nice to meet you
You and your partner are meeting for the first time. You want to get to know each other and find out what you have in common. Ask and answer appropriate questions and comment on each other's answers. The questions below will give you some ideas.

Example
What kind of music do you like? -> I like jazz. -> So do I. / Oh, I don't I prefer heavy metal.

What kind of music do you like?   Are you a student?   What is your favourite food?
Do you like going to the cinema?   Which countries have you been to?
Where do you go on holiday?   Have you ever been to California?

UNIT 3
'This is easy, isn't it?'

> You like Japanese food, don't you?

> Yes, I do. I really love sushi. You've eaten sushi before, haven't you?

> Yes, I have. I used to live in Tokyo. You've never been to Tokyo, have you?

> No, I haven't. But I've been to Okinawa. You've been there, too, haven't you?

> Yes, I've been there twice. It's a beautiful city, isn't it?

Question tags

Question tags have a variety of uses – to steer a conversation, seek agreement or indicate an expected answer. Question tags help to make a conversation flow. For example, instead of saying 'Is this lesson too easy?' or 'Do you think this lesson is too easy?', we can say, 'This lesson is too easy, isn't it?'

The tense of the verb in the question tag matches the tense of the verb in the preceding sentence.

The question tag is added to the end of a sentence. If the sentence is affirmative, the question tag is negative. If the sentence is negative, the question tag is affirmative. If the verb in the first sentence is affirmative but the sentence includes the words *seldom*, *rarely*, or *hardly*, an affirmative question tag is used.

> The film wasn't very good, was it?

> I thought it was OK. You don't like action movies, do you?

> Not really, but I like Brad Walker. You saw him in Star Rage 2, didn't you?

> Yes, I did. It was great, wasn't it?

> It's very dry today, isn't it?

> Well, it rarely rains in summer, does it?

> You're going to the dance with Sally, aren't you?

> You know a lot about my private life, don't you?

18

SPEAKING ACTIVITIES 3

1 Grammar Drills
Practice with a partner. **Student A**, go to page 40. **Student B**, go to page 62.

2 I've heard a lot about you
You and your partner are both attending a gala dinner. You have never met before, but once you find out each other's names, you think you have heard about them before. Ask questions to check the information. Use the sentences below and continue with some of your own.

Example
You're from France, aren't you?

You're from France   You used to live in London   You graduated from Oxford

You're married to a film star   You have spent some time in China

You work at the embassy   You like fast cars   You know my brother

You were at school with the prime minister   You won a gold medal

You can speak three languages   You made a TV documentary

3 Caught red-handed
A shoplifter has been arrested. You and your partner are detectives. Take it in turns to ask the suspect questions based on the information below.

Example
You entered the department store at 12:15 pm, didn't you?

The suspect entered the department store at 12:15 pm. They were wearing a dark blue track suit and a baseball cap. They were carrying a large shopping bag. They took several items off the shelf and placed them in the bag. They did not see the security camera, but they were captured on video. They took a cheap T-shirt from a hanger. Then they went to the checkout and paid for the T-shirt. They did not pay for the items in the bag. They left the shop at 12:30 pm.

UNIT 4
'The lesson was cancelled.'

Yesterday's English lesson was cancelled.

Oh, really? Were you told in advance?

Yes, we were told by the teacher that the timetable had been changed.

I see. And have our papers been marked?

No. they will be marked next week.

Who will they be marked by?

By the head of department.

Passive sentences

The passive can be used to focus on the object of an action and to avoid mentioning the subject. The object can be a direct or indirect object.

The object of an active sentence becomes the subject of the passive sentence. The verb **to be** is used as an auxiliary verb followed by the past participle of the main verb.

The original subject can be introduced by the word **by**. This comes after the verb.

The project was completed on time.

Did you complete it yourself?

Who will submit the final draft?

No, it was completed by a team of six.

It will be submitted by the team leader.

I have been awarded a book prize.

That's great news! Who will the prize be presented by?

The prize will be presented by the mayor.

SPEAKING ACTIVITIES 4

1 Grammar Drills
Practice with a partner. **Student A**, go to page 42. **Student B**, go to page 64.

2 I shot the sheriff
Take turns to read and correct the sentences below, using a passive form in each case. Then make up some sentences of your own and do the same.

Example

I shot the sheriff. (an outlaw) -> No, the sheriff was shot by an outlaw.

> I shot the sheriff. (an outlaw)
> The baker sells meat. (the butcher)
> You scratched my car. (someone else)
> The boss answers the telephone. (an assistant)
> The doctor changes the bandages. (a nurse)
> The driver services the engine. (a mechanic)
> Her mother cuts her hair. (her hairdresser)
> Lord Staines opens the door. (his butler)

3 The Black Phantom
A number of crimes have been committed in Comic City. The police are questioning everybody in the area. Take turns to ask each other questions and to explain to the police that all the following crimes were committed by the evil Black Phantom. In each case, choose the correct verb from the box to form a passive sentence.

Example

Did you blow up the mayor's car? -> No, I didn't. It was blown up by the Black Phantom.

> *mayor's car*
> governess's diamonds
> City Hall
> First City Bank
> governor's residence
> precious painting by van Kruft
> power station
> mayor's daughter

sabotage	kidnap
steal	*blow up*
damage	
burgle burn down	rob

UNIT 5
'I'm really excited.'

I am really excited about the new video game.

I'm not. I think video games are boring. Action movies are more exciting.

Oh, no. I'm always bored by movies. I like to be part of the action.

I see. But don't you think that some movies are shocking?

No, I'm not easily shocked.

Participle adjectives

Participle adjectives take the same form as past participles (**bored**, **interested**, **shocked**) and present participles (**boring**, **interesting**, and **shocking**).

Past participle adjectives often express emotions experienced by the subject of the sentence or clause.

Present participle adjectives express properties of the subject.

I am very interested in English. It's my favourite subject.

Hasenmayer's new symphony is so exciting.

I am annoyed. I study so hard, but I am never satisfied with my grade.

I think classical music is boring.

Don't be depressed. Your teacher was pleased by your test results.

I suppose you find vegan pop more interesting. I find it depressing.

Yes, I was surprised by that.

That's surprising. It can be very uplifting.

SPEAKING ACTIVITIES 5

1 Grammar Drills
Practice with a partner. **Student A**, go to page 44. **Student B**, go to page 66.

2 Springboard questions
Look at the list of questions below. Take turns to choose a question from the list and use the question to spark off a brief discussion.

<u>Example</u>
A: *Which TV shows are you interested in?*
B: *Well, I'm interested in classic movies, but documentaries are interesting, too.*
   What about you? What kind of shows are you interested in?
A: *I find old movies boring, but some documentaries can be really fascinating.*

1. Which TV shows are you interested in?
2. Which news topics do you find boring?
3. Is there anything you are terrified of?
4. What job would you find exciting?
5. What do you find annoying?
6. What was the last time you were worried?
7. What kinds of hobbies do you think are relaxing?
8. Have you ever been very embarrassed?
9. Which sports are the most challenging?
10. Which foods are you disgusted by?
11. Which habits are most annoying?
12. What makes you frustrated?
13. Which type of exercise do you find exhausting?
14. What do you do to feel relaxed?
15. What makes you feel energized?
16. Which celebrities are most entertaining?
17. Which animals do you think are frightening?
18. When was the last time you saw something fascinating?
19. Have you ever felt overwhelmed?
20. Who is the most inspiring person in your life?

UNIT 6
'I'm older than you.'

> Your exam results were better than mine.

> Yes, but I'm older than you.

> That doesn't mean you're more intelligent than me.

> No, of course not. But anyway, the exam was easier than last year.

> Really? I thought it was more difficult.

Comparative adjectives

Comparative adjectives are used to compare two nouns ('Physics is harder than English') or noun phrases ('The test we took last year...'). They are also used in comparative clauses ('My score was higher than I expected').

Some adjectives become comparative adjectives by adding **-er** to the end of the adjective. This applies to all one-syllable adjectives (e.g. **tall**, **short**, **quick**) and two-syllable adjectives ending in **-er**, **-le**, or **-ow** (e.g. **clever**, **gentle**, **narrow**). With two-syllable adjectives ending in **-y** (e.g. **happy**, **pretty**, **easy**), **-y** is replaced by **-ier**. Other two-syllable adjectives and adjectives with three or more syllables receive **more** before the adjective.

There are five irregular adjectives:
good -> **better**, **bad** -> **worse**, **far** -> **farther**, **little** -> **less**, **many** -> **more**.

If there is a big difference between the two things being compared, the words **much**, **a lot**, **far** or **so much** can be used. If there is only a small difference, the words **slightly**, **a bit** or **not much** can be used.

> The test was simpler than I expected.

> Yes, I hope my score is higher than it was last time.

> These dresses are more beautiful than the other ones.

> Yes, but they are also more expensive.

> I think Greek is harder to learn than English.

> Yes, but Greek is easier than Chinese.

> I know. You are slightly younger than my mother.

> I'm much older than you.

SPEAKING ACTIVITIES 6

1 Grammar Drills
Practice with a partner. **Student A**, go to page 46. **Student B**, go to page 68.

2 A presidential debate
You and your partner are candidates for the presidency of the country you are in. During a presidential debate, each candidate compares themselves favourably to the other one. Use the adjectives from the box and add some of your own.

Example
I'm smarter than he/she is.

smart   mature   healthy   confident responsible   educated   dependable   charismatic honest   reliable   strong   fit

3 The other candidate
Now compare the other candidate to yourself. Use the adjectives from the box and add some of your own.

Example
He/she's more corrupt than I am.

4 A happy honeymoon
You and your partner have been asked to help a young couple choose a destination for their honeymoon. Compare the two options below using the adjectives given and add some of your own.

Example
They could stay at the Paradiso because it's more relaxing.
- Yes, but the Grand Palace is more luxurious.

Paradiso	Grand Palace
relaxing convenient near cheap traditional	exotic far away expensive *luxurious* spacious

UNIT 7
'I'm the fastest.'

Did you know that Russia is the biggest country in the world?

Yes, but did you know that Lake Baikal is the deepest lake in the world?

Of course. It's also one of the clearest lakes on Earth.

Yes, and I think it's the most ancient lake, too.

Superlative adjectives

Superlative adjectives are mainly used to compare one noun to a group of nouns. They can also be used in relative clauses.

Some adjectives become superlative adjectives by adding *-est* to the end of the adjective. This applies to all one-syllable adjectives (e.g. *tall*, *short*, *quick*) and two-syllable adjectives ending in *-er*, *-le*, or *-ow* (e.g. *clever*, *gentle*, *narrow*). With two-syllable adjectives ending in *-y* (e.g. *happy*, *pretty*, *easy*), *-y* is replaced by *-iest*. Other two-syllable adjectives and adjectives with three or more syllables receive *most* before the adjective.

There are five irregular adjectives:
good -> *best*, *bad* -> *worst*, *far* -> *farthest*, *little* -> *least*, *many* -> *most*.

You're not the most skilful player in our team.

No, but I'm the fastest runner.

She's the most beautiful woman I have ever seen.

If you marry me, I'll be the happiest woman in the world.

Yes, and she wears the most expensive clothes you can buy.

And I'll be the luckiest man in the world.

This restaurant serves the best food in town.

Is this the longest road in the town?

Yes, but it has the worst service.

Yes, it's also the narrowest.

SPEAKING ACTIVITIES 7

1 Grammar Drills
Practice with a partner. **Student A**, go to page 48. **Student B**, go to page 70.

2 Friends and family
Take turns with a partner to complete the sentence, 'Out of my friends and family, the
_____ person is _____', using a superlative
adjective formed from one of the words below in the first blank and a friend or a family
member's name in the second blank.

considerate	enthusiastic	clever	awesome
punctual	friendly	rich	brave
calm	helpful	creative	happy
wise	poor	romantic	stupid
athletic	popular	old	
artistic	lazy	lucky	
outgoing	honest	crazy	

3 A blind date
Try to persuade your partner to go on a blind date with someone. Describe the person
using the superlative forms of the adjectives below, or use adjectives of your own.

sexy	beautiful	handsome	hilarious
strong	charming	rich	funny
exciting	positive	fun	smart
tall	romantic	cute	

UNIT 8
'It's hard to study all night.'

> It is hard to study all night.

> I know. That is why it is smart to study for a week before the exam.

> That's true. But it is crazy to expect me to study seven days before the exam.

> I studied for a week. It wasn't so hard. And today it was easy to take the exam.

Dummy subjects

Dummy subjects are often used when there is no subject attached to the verb. For example, when we say, 'It is raining', or 'It is twelve o'clock', the word *it* is a dummy subject. Similarly, in the sentence, 'There are three restaurants in the high street', the word *there* is a dummy subject. We also use a dummy subject to avoid using a long verbal phrase as a subject.

Sometimes we need to change a gerund (e.g. *living*) to an infinitive (e.g. *to live*).

Instead of saying...	we say...
To drive to Paris takes a long time.	It takes a long time to drive to Paris.
That you had an extra ticket was very fortunate.	It was very fortunate that you had an extra ticket.
The fact that the store is closed on Sundays is inconvenient.	It is inconvenient that the store is closed on Sundays.
Arriving early for class is always a good idea.	It is always a good idea to arrive early for class.
Living on Jupiter is impossible.	It is impossible to live on Jupiter.

> Why do you always drive to work?

> Because it's too far to walk.

> Science can be really confusing.

> I know. It's not easy to understand quantum physics.

> Can you give me any tips about hiking in the mountains?

> Yes. It's important to wear the right clothing.

> This study guide is very good.

> Yes, there are a lot of useful tips in it.

SPEAKING ACTIVITIES 8

1 Grammar Drills

Practice with a partner. **Student A**, go to page 50. **Student B**, go to page 72.

2 What do you think?

With a partner, take turns to complete the sentences below and then say what you think about each topic.

1. It is not easy to…
2. It is a pity that I…
3. It is fun to…
4. When studying a foreign language, it is important to…
5. It is hard to…
6. I have always thought it is interesting that…
7. It is not good for your health to…
8. It is impossible to…
9. I have always thought it was a good idea to…
10. I think it is a waste of time to…
11. When I was a high school student, it was embarrassing that…
12. I think it is obvious that…
13. It is doubtful that…
14. It is very convenient that…
15. It is surprising that…
16. It was so unfortunate that…
17. It is disappointing that…
18. It is always fun to…
19. It is too difficult to…
20. It is very confusing to…

3 It's hard to say.

Discuss the following questions with your partner. If you are not sure about something, begin with *It's hard to say*, then give your opinion. Add some questions of your own.

Is there life in outer space? Are there enough restaurants in your town?
Should there be more hospitals in your country? Are there too many cars on the roads?
Why are there so many airlines? Will there ever be enough food for everyone?

29

UNIT 9
'It was Marlowe who wrote that.'

Shakespeare wrote Edward II.

No, it was Marlowe who wrote Edward II.

Did Professor Steiner tell you that?

No, it was Professor Mao who told me that last week.

But I thought you didn't like Renaissance drama.

I don't. It's the language that makes the plays difficult to read.

It-cleft sentences for emphasis

It-cleft sentences are commonly used to correct an incorrect statement.

This type of sentence begins with **It** followed by the appropriate form of the verb **to be**. This is then followed by the part of the sentence that is being corrected.

After the information that is being corrected, **that** is commonly used.

If the information that is being corrected is a person or a group of persons, **who** can be used instead of **that**. If time is involved, we can use **when**.

Canada is the largest country.

No. It's Russia that's the largest country.

They went to Berlin last year.

No, it was Frankfurt that they went to last year.

Dr Jones studied economics.

No. It was political science that Dr Jones studied.

Pizza comes from France.

I don't think so. It is Italy where Pizza comes from.

John married Sally last year.

It wasn't Sally who John married. It was Mary.

Pierre married Yvonne last year.

It was two years ago when Pierre married Yvonne.

30

SPEAKING ACTIVITIES 9

1 Grammar Drills

Practice with a partner. **Student A**, go to page 52. **Student B**, go to page 74.

2 Oh, no, it isn't!

All the statements in the list below are incorrect. Taking turns, one partner reads out a statement and the other corrects it as shown in the example. Base your answer on the correct information given in the box.

Example

Mars is larger than Earth.   *Oh, no, it isn't! It is Venus that is larger than Mars.*

Mars is larger than Venus.

Starry Night was painted by Leonardo da Vinci.

The Mona Lisa was painted by Van Gogh.

The first Harry Potter book was published in 1998.

Cricket is the national sport of Scotland

The Great Pyramid of Giza is located in Peru.

Stonehenge is located in Wales.

The Eiffel Tower was completed in 1898.

The Titanic sank in 1911.

Shakespeare was born in 1654.

The Mona Lisa was painted by Leonardo da Vinci.	Starry Night was painted by Van Gogh.
Venus is larger than Mars.	The first Harry Potter book was published in 1997.
Golf is the national sport of Scotland	The Great Pyramid of Giza is located in Egypt.
Stonehenge is located in England.	The Eiffel Tower was completed in 1889.
The Titanic sank in 1912.	Shakespeare was born in 1564.

3 True or false

On a separate piece of paper, write down three true statements (e.g. *Paris is the capital of France*) and three false statements (e.g. *Christmas Day is on 31 December*). Then take turns to read out the statements. The other person should respond *"That's right"* if the statement is true or use a cleft sentence to correct a statement that is false.

UNIT 10
'He wears white cotton shirts.'

> I want a boyfriend, and since I am French, I want a French boyfriend.

> I bet you want a good-looking French boyfriend.

> Of course. Actually, I want a generous, good-looking French boyfriend.

> But that sounds just like your last boyfriend.

> Well then, I want a new generous, good-looking French boyfriend.

Adjective order

When two or more adjectives are placed before a noun, the adjectives tend to be in a specific order. Sometimes the order of the adjectives can be changed for emphasis, with the emphasised adjective coming sooner in the sentence, but if there is no special emphasis, the order is usually as shown below. The table shows examples only.

1	Opinion	great, amazing, easy, difficult, beautiful, ugly, friendly, lovely, nice, cute, delicious
2	Size	little, big, large, tall, short, tiny, enormous, fat
3	Shape	round, square, circular, rectangular, long, tight
4	Condition	clean, wet, rich, hungry, classic, hot, expensive,
5	Age	young, old, ancient, mature, teenage, modern, new, classic
6	Colour	black, white, red, green, blue, purple, yellow
7	Pattern	striped, plain, dotted, spotted
8	Origin	French, Japanese, Egyptian, Indian, Irish, Eastern, Scottish
9	Material	wooden, plastic, metal, cotton, silk, gold, leather, glass, stone
10	Type	gardening, sleeping, roasting, shopping, driving, winter, terraced, sports, business

> Do you think Gavin will like this red silk shirt?

> Do you like the decor of this old Georgian terraced house?

> No, he always wears white cotton shirts.

> Yes, especially the green striped wallpaper and that amazing polished-brass door knocker.

> What sort of shoes are you looking for?

> What's the new exchange student like?

> I need a pair of strong, leather running shoes.

> She's a beautiful slim dark-haired Moroccan girl.

SPEAKING ACTIVITIES 10

1 Grammar Drills

Practice with a partner. **Student A**, go to page 54. **Student B**, go to page 76.

2 Tell me more

Work with a partner. For each item listed below, ask and give information as shown in the example. Use as many adjectives as you can. Add some of your own

Example

A: *What can you tell me about the car?*
B: *It's a red car.*
A: *Tell me more.*
B: *It's a big red car.*
A: *Tell me more*
B: *It's a big red American car.*
A: *Tell me more…*

| **Car:** | modern/classic/custom | new/second-hand | big/compact/small |
| | red/black/silver | American/German/Japanese | fast/economical/powerful |

| **Sofa:** | leather/cotton/synthetic | antique/modern/fashionable | |
| | striped/patterned/plain | two-seater/three-seater | white/brown/grey |

| **House:** | small/spacious/enormous | detached/semi-detached/terraced | |
| | stone/timber/brick | town/country single-storey/two-storey/three-storey | |

| **Gloves:** | silk/woollen/kid | elegant/fashionable/practical | thick/thin/warm |
| | gardening/driving/winter | green/black/blue | Italian/Chinese/Mexican |

3 Sales patter

One partner takes the role of a salesperson and the other that of a customer. The customer asks about a product, then the salesperson offers a choice of models and makes a recommendation. Keep swapping roles until all the products have been described.

Example

A: *Which TV would you recommend?*
B: *Well, I can offer you a small black Japanese TV, but I would actually recommend a large silver Korean model instead.*

| T-shirt | TV | mobile phone | microwave oven | watch |
| jeans | shoes | rucksack | computer | bicycle |

33

PART TWO
Grammar Drills – Student A

Unit 1 Grammar Drills Student A

You are Student A. Your partner is Student B. Read Student A's statement number 1. Student B will listen and ask a question indicating surprising information. Check Student B's response. Then Student B will read sentence number 2 and you must listen and ask a question indicating surprising information. Repeat the procedure for all statements.

Student A

Student B

1
I can speak 30 languages.

How many languages can you speak?

3
I forgot to go to my wedding.

Where did you forget to go?

5
I won the lottery yesterday.

What did you win yesterday?

7
Some Gucci bags cost 10,000 dollars.

How much do some Gucci bags cost?

9
I ate 12 pieces of pizza last night.

How many pieces of pizza did you eat last night?

11

I want to be Secretary General of the United Nations.

What do you want to be?

13

I climbed Mount Everest last year.

What did you climb last year?

15

I woke up at 3 o'clock this morning.

What time did you wake up this morning?

17

I sold my car for 50,000 dollars.

How much did you sell your car for?

19

My friend can type 100 words per minute.

How many words per minute can your friend type?

21

My brother has travelled to Cuba fifty times.

How many times has your brother travelled to Cuba?

23

I used to work at the White House.

Where did you use to work?

Unit 2 Grammar Drills Student A

You are Student A. Your partner is Student B. Look at the mini-dialogue in number 1. Read Student A's words to Student B. Student B will try to say the correct phrase to complete the dialogue. Check Student B's response and correct it if necessary. Then swap roles for number 2. Proceed in the same way for all the mini-dialogues.

Student A   **Student B**

1   I'm from Japan.

So am I.   I was born in Tokyo.

2   (listen)

_____ I went to London and Manchester.

3   I'll have a sandwich.

I won't.   I want something else.

4   (listen)

_____ I eat it once a week.

5   My sister helps me with my

Mine doesn't.   She says I should do it

6   (listen)

_____ The classes are too difficult.

7   My mother always told me to study hard.

My mother didn't.   She didn't care about my grades.

38

Student A   **Student B**

8   (listen)

_____ I learned when I was young.

9 My father has never washed the dishes.

Neither has my father. My mother thinks he is lazy.

10   (listen)

_____ I think she is absolutely right.

11 I won't take a job this vacation.

Neither will I. I don't need the money.

12   (listen)

_____ I went to lots of concerts.

13 I'm going to the Olympics next year.

So am I. That is quite a coincidence.

14   (listen)

_____ I'm going to Moscow.

15 I don't understand nuclear physics.

Neither do I. It's too hard.

Unit 3 Grammar Drills Student A

Read out the first sentence but do not read out the question tag. Your partner will try to complete the sentence with the correct question tag. Check their response against the question tag in brackets. Then your partner will read out the next sentence. Listen and try to complete the sentence with the correct question tag. Your partner will check your response. Repeat for all 30 sentences and question tags.

1. **Your name is John,**   (isn't it?)

2. (Listen to your partner and add the correct question tag.)

3. **You can eat spicy food,**   (can't you?)

4. (Listen to your partner and add the correct question tag.)

5. **Their son never studies hard,**   (does he?)

6. (Listen to your partner and add the correct question tag.)

7. **It was windy this morning,**   (wasn't it?)

8. (Listen to your partner and add the correct question tag.)

9. **This class is really interesting,**   (isn't it?)

10. (Listen to your partner and add the correct question tag.)

11. **You rarely speak to him,**   (do you?)

12. (Listen to your partner and add the correct question tag.)

13. **It's three o'clock,**   (isn't it?)

14. (Listen to your partner and add the correct question tag.)

15. **You were talking to him,** (weren't you?)

16. (Listen to your partner and add the correct question tag.)

17. **You don't remember my name,** (do you?)

18. (Listen to your partner and add the correct question tag.)

19. **He didn't know what he was doing,** (did he?)

20. (Listen to your partner and add the correct question tag.)

21. **She's your friend,** (isn't she?)

22. (Listen to your partner and add the correct question tag.)

23. **I'm not going to get full marks in the English test,** (am I?)

24. (Listen to your partner and add the correct question tag.)

25. **Jupiter is larger than Mars,** (isn't it?)

26. (Listen to your partner and add the correct question tag.)

27. **You're not allergic to seafood,** (are you?)

28. (Listen to your partner and add the correct question tag.)

29. **She can't speak Japanese,** (can she?)

30. (Listen to your partner and add the correct question tag.)

Unit 4 Grammar Drills Student A

With your partner, take turns to convert the sentences below from active to passive or from passive to active. For each of the even-numbered sentences, read out the version in **bold type**. Your partner will then convert it from active to passive or from passive to active as appropriate. Your partner will read out the odd-numbered sentences for you to convert from active to passive or from passive to active.

	Active	Passive
1	**Every day, Michael cooks breakfast.**	Every day, breakfast is cooked by Michael.
2	(Listen and respond)	
3	Right now, Ditta is repairing my bike.	**Right now, my bike is being repaired by Ditta.**
4	(Listen and respond)	
5	**Recently, her husband has done all the housework.**	Recently, all the housework has been done by her husband.
6	(Listen and respond)	
7	Her father used to pay her mortgage.	**Her mortgage used to be paid by her father.**
8	(Listen and respond)	
9	**My parents would always make my friends welcome.**	My friends would always be made welcome by my parents.
10	(Listen and respond)	
11	I thought the president would win the election.	**I thought the election would be won by the president.**

12	(Listen and respond)	
13	**A teenager wearing blue jeans and a red shirt stole my bike.**	My bike was stolen by a teenager wearing blue jeans and red shirt.
14	(Listen and respond)	
15	Over two thousand people read his tweets every day.	**His tweets are read by over two thousand people every day.**
16	(Listen and respond)	
17	**The AcroSoft corporation has fired a hundred office workers.**	A hundred office workers have been fired by the AcroSoft corporation.
18	(Listen and respond)	
19	Mary changed the flat tyre.	**The flat tyre was changed by Mary.**
20	(Listen and respond)	
21	**John Wilkes Booth assassinated Abraham Lincoln.**	Abraham Lincoln was assassinated by John Wilkes Booth.
22	(Listen and respond)	
23	Seawater corroded the metal supports.	**The metal supports were corroded by seawater.**
24	(Listen and respond)	
25	**A forest fire destroyed the village.**	The village was destroyed by a forest fire.
26	(Listen and respond)	

Unit 5 Grammar Drills Student A

With your partner, take turns to solve the tasks below. For each odd-numbered sentence, read out the *prompt verb* and the sentence that follows it. Your partner will repeat the sentence and try to replace the word **what** with the correct participle formed from the prompt verb. Check your partner's answer against the key. For the even-numbered questions, your partner will read out the *prompt verb* and a sentence. Repeat the sentence you hear and try to replace the word **what** with the correct participle formed from the prompt verb. Your partner will check your answer.

1. *Excite*   Skydiving is very **what**.
   Key: Skydiving is very **exciting**.

2. *Surprise*

3. *Interest*   Jenny thinks art is very **what**.
   Key: Jenny thinks art is very **interesting**.

4. *Shock*

5. *Confuse*   Many students are **what** by calculus.
   Key: Many students are **confused** by calculus.

6. *Disappoint*

7. *Exhaust*   He was **what** by the marathon.
   Key: He was **exhausted** by the marathon.

8. *Thrill*

9. *Amaze*   Michael Jordan was **what** at basketball.
   Key: Michael Jordan was **amazing** at basketball.

10. *Depress*

11. *Entertain*   Musicals are usually very **what**.
    Key: Musicals are usually very **entertaining**.

12. *Convince*

13. *Relax*   I feel very **what** after a hot bath.
    Key: I feel very **relaxed** after a hot bath.

44

14. *Tire*

15. *Disgust*   He was **what** by the terrible mess in the kitchen.
    Key: He was **disgusted** by the terrible mess in the kitchen.

16. *Amaze*

17. *Embarrass*   It was **what** to talk to her.
    Key: It was **embarrassing** to talk to her.

18. *Frighten*

19. *Bore*   The students were never **what** in his class.
    Key: The students were never **bored** in his class.

20. *Fascinate*

21. *Challenge*   Taking part in this race was very **what**.
    Key: Taking part in this race was very **challenging**.

22. *Confuse*

23. *Threaten*   The boy felt **what** by the dark shape coming toward him.
    Key: The boy felt **threatened** by the dark shape coming toward him.

24. *Satisfy*

25. *Amuse*   The comedy was highly **what**.
    Key: The comedy was highly **amusing**.

26. *Annoy*

27. *Worry*   The weather forecast looks very **what**.
    Key: The weather forecast looks very **worrying**.

28. *Relax*

29. *Tire*   He is usually **what** at the end of the day.
    Key: He is usually **tired** at the end of the day.

30. *Exhaust*

Unit 6 Grammar Drills Student A

With your partner, take turns to solve the tasks below. For each odd-numbered sentence, read out the *prompt adjective* and the sentence that follows it. Your partner will repeat the sentence and try to replace the word **what** with the correct comparative formed from the prompt adjective. Check your partner's answer against the key. For the even-numbered questions, your partner will read out the *prompt adjective* and a sentence. Repeat the sentence you hear and try to replace the word **what** with the correct comparative formed from the prompt adjective. Your partner will check your answer.

1. *strange*   Artists have **what** personalities than other people.
   Key: Artists have **stranger** personalities than other people.

2. *modern*

3. *comfortable* My new sofa is **what** than my old sofa.
   Key: My new sofa is **more comfortable** than my old sofa.

4. *important*

5. *safe*   My hometown is **what** than Paris.
   Key: My hometown is **safer** than Paris.

6. *dirty*

7. *flat*   Holland is much **what** than Nepal.
   Key: Holland is much **flatter** than Nepal.

8. *careful*

9. *hungry*   I am much **what** then you are.
   Key: I am much **hungrier** than you are.

10. *noisy*

11. *expensive* Gucci is **what** than other brands.
    Key: Gucci is **more expensive** than other brands.

12. *bad*

13. *heavy*   A truck is much **what** than a compact car.
    Key: A truck is much **heavier** than a compact car.

14. *thin*

15. *exotic* The Jungle Palace restaurant is much **what** than the Tivoli.
    Key: The Jungle Palace restaurant is much **more exotic** than the Tivoli.

16. *popular*

17. *large* Russia is so much **what** than North Korea.
    Key: Russia is so much **larger** than North Korea.

18. *good*

19. *happy* I am much **what** now than when I was in high school.
    Key: I am much **happier** now than when I was in high school.

20. *sweet*

21. *handsome* Her new boyfriend is a lot **what** than her ex-boyfriend.
    Key: Her new boyfriend is a lot **more handsome** than her ex-boyfriend.

22. *exciting*

23. *lucky* He is **what** by far than I am.
    Key: He is **luckier** by far than I am.

24. *tall*

25. *afraid* He's **what** of spiders than of snakes.
    Key: He's **more afraid** of spiders than of snakes.

26. *long*

27. *fast* A cheetah is much **what** than a tiger.
    Key: A cheetah is much **faster** than a tiger.

28. *intense*

29. *cool* Today, the weather is **what** than it was yesterday.
    Key: Today, the weather is **cooler** than it was yesterday.

30. *high*

Unit 7 Grammar Drills Student A

With your partner, take turns to solve the tasks below. For each odd-numbered task, read out the prompt. Your partner will try to form a sentence using the correct superlative form of the adjective in the prompt. Check your partner's answer against the key. For the even-numbered tasks, your partner will read out the prompt. Listen and try to form a sentence using the correct superlative form of the adjective in the prompt. Your partner will check your answer.

	Prompt	Key
1	**Mount Everest / tall / mountain**	Mount Everest is the tallest mountain.
2	(Listen and respond)	
3	**Summer / hot / season**	Summer is the hottest season.
4	(Listen and respond)	
5	**Paris / romantic / city**	Paris is the most romantic city.
6	(Listen and respond)	
7	**February / short / month**	February is the shortest month.
8	(Listen and respond)	
9	**Astrophysics / difficult / subject**	Astrophysics is the most difficult subject.
10	(Listen and respond)	
11	**Brian Bantu / fast / swimmer**	Brian Bantu is the fastest swimmer.
12	(Listen and respond)	
13	**The new Lamborghini / expensive / car**	The new Lamborghini is the most expensive car.

14	(Listen and respond)	
15	**Jupiter / large / planet**	Jupiter is the largest planet.
16	(Listen and respond)	
17	**Giraffes / long / necks**	Giraffes have the longest necks.
18	(Listen and respond)	
19	**Thirteen / unlucky / number**	Thirteen is the unluckiest number.
20	(Listen and respond)	
21	**The reigning champion / good / boxer**	The reigning champion is the best boxer.
22	(Listen and respond)	
23	**Machu Picchu / impressive / holiday destination**	Machu Picchu is the most impressive holiday destination.
24	(Listen and respond)	
25	**Shambles Alley / narrow / street**	Shambles Alley is the narrowest street.
26	(Listen and respond)	
27	**Supremo New Blend / creamy / coffee**	Supremo New Blend is the creamiest coffee.
28	(Listen and respond)	
29	**Football / popular / sport**	Football is the most popular sport.
30	(Listen and respond)	

Unit 8 Grammar Drills Student A

With your partner, take turns to solve the tasks below. For each odd-numbered task, read out the prompt. Your partner will try to reformulate the prompt using a dummy subject. Check your partner's answer against the key. For the even-numbered tasks, your partner will read out the prompt. Listen and try to reformulate the prompt using a dummy subject. Your partner will check your answer.

	Prompt	Key
1	**To read mystery novels is fun.**	It's fun to read mystery novels.
2	(Listen and respond)	
3	**To find out about your parents' childhood is interesting.**	It's interesting to find out about your parents' childhood.
4	(Listen and respond)	
5	**To drink and drive is never a good idea.**	It's never a good idea to drink and drive.
6	(Listen and respond)	
7	**Wearing safety equipment is important.**	It's important to wear safety equipment.
8	(Listen and respond)	
9	**Being on time is always a good policy.**	It's always a good policy to be on time.
10	(Listen and respond)	
11	**That I burned the dinner was embarrassing.**	It was embarrassing that I burned the dinner.
12	(Listen and respond)	
13	**Running a marathon in the summer isn't easy.**	It isn't easy to run a marathon in the summer.

14	(Listen and respond)	
15	**Whether the injured athlete will take part in the Olympic Games is doubtful.**	It's doubtful whether the injured athlete will take part in the Olympic Games.
16	(Listen and respond)	
17	**That you had an extra ticket was fortunate.**	It was fortunate that you had an extra ticket
18	(Listen and respond)	
19	**To live on Jupiter is impossible.**	It's impossible to live on Jupiter.
20	(Listen and respond)	
21	**To be helpful to others is a great thing.**	It's a great thing to be helpful to others.
22	(Listen and respond)	
23	**That Jenny Tardy always comes to class late is disrespectful.**	It's disrespectful that Jenny Tardy always comes to class late.
24	(Listen and respond)	
25	**That there is so much hunger in the world is hard to believe.**	It's hard to believe that there is so much hunger in the world.
26	(Listen and respond)	
27	**That so few people go to the theatre nowadays is a sad reflection on society.**	It's a sad reflection on society that so few people go to the theatre nowadays.
28	(Listen and respond)	
29	**Talking is good.**	It's good to talk.
30	(Listen and respond)	

Unit 9 Grammar Drills Student A

First, read out the information in box 1, repeating it if necessary. Then read out sentence 1a and check your partner's response. Then read out sentence 1b and check your partner's response. Then swap roles for number 2 and continue until all the tasks are completed.

1	John and Michael were brothers. John was tall, strong and dark-haired. Michael was short, fragile and blonde, but Michael was very smart.	
1a	**John was short.**	No, it's Michael who was short.
1b	**Michael was very smart.**	That's right!
2	(Listen and respond)	
3	Christopher Columbus was an explorer who sailed across the Atlantic Ocean. He was born in Genoa, Italy in 1451 and died in Valladolid, Spain in 1506.	
3a	**Christopher Columbus was born in Spain.**	No, it was Italy where Christopher Columbus was born.
3b	**Christopher Columbus was born in 1451.**	That's right!
4	(Listen and respond)	
5	Mount Everest is the tallest mountain in the world. It is located in the Himalayan mountain range. In 1953, Sir Edmund Hillary and Tenzing Norgay were the first people to climb the mountain.	
5a	**Everest is the tallest mountain in the Himalayan mountain range.**	That's right!
5b	**Everest was first climbed in 1950.**	No, it was 1953 when Everest was first climbed.
6	(Listen and respond)	

7	Biology and botany are both scientific disciplines. Biology is the study of all living organisms, Botany is the study of plants. Zoology is the study of the animal kingdom.	
7a	**Botany is the study of animals.**	No, it's zoology that is the study of animals.
7b	**Biology is the study of all living organisms.**	That's right!
8	(Listen and respond)	
9	Arthur Miller and George Bernard Shaw were both dramatists. Arthur Miller was born in New York in 1915. George Bernard Shaw was born in Dublin in 1856. Arthur Miller wrote The Crucible. George Bernard Shaw wrote Arms and The Man.	
9a	**Arthur Miller was born in New Jersey.**	No, it was New York where Arthur Miller was born.
9b	**George Bernard Shaw was the dramatist who wrote Arms and The Man.**	That's right!
10	(Listen and respond)	
11	The Parthenon and the Pantheon are both ancient monuments. The Parthenon is located in Athens. The Pantheon is in Rome and was built as a temple dedicated to all gods.	
11a	**The Parthenon was dedicated to all gods.**	No, it's the Pantheon that was dedicated to all gods
11b	**The Pantheon is in Rome.**	That's right!
12	(Listen and respond)	
13	When the Titanic sank in 1912, it was a major maritime disaster. Over a thousand people died when the ship hit an iceberg.	
13a	**The disaster occurred in 1912.**	That's right!
13b	**About five hundred people died.**	No, it was over a thousand people that died.
14	(Listen and respond)	

Unit 10 Grammar Drills Student A

With your partner, take turns to solve the tasks below. For each odd-numbered task, read out the prompt. Your partner will try to form a sentence using the correct adjective order. Check your partner's answer against the key. For the even-numbered tasks, your partner will read out the prompt. Listen and try to form a sentence using the correct adjective order. Your partner will check your answer.

	Prompt	Key
1	I always wear shirts that are cotton and green.	I always wear green cotton shirts.
2	(Listen and respond)	
3	Her boyfriend was a man who was friendly and young.	Her boyfriend was a friendly young man.
4	(Listen and respond)	
5	My son wants a dog that is black, big and lovely.	My son wants a lovely big black dog.
6	(Listen and respond)	
7	I used to drive a sports car that was classic and red.	I used to drive a classic red sports car.
8	(Listen and respond)	
9	My favourite movie is a film that is old and French.	My favourite movie is an old French film.
10	(Listen and respond)	
11	The vacation I had in the summer break was nice and long.	In the summer break I had a nice long vacation.

12	(Listen and respond)	
13	**I am from a village that is charming and old.**	I am from a charming old village.
14	(Listen and respond)	
15	**I ordered the vegetable soup that is delicious and hot.**	I ordered the delicious hot vegetable soup.
16	(Listen and respond)	
17	**My girlfriend has hair that is long, brown and beautiful.**	My girlfriend has beautiful long brown hair.
18	(Listen and respond)	
19	**The receptionist is a woman who is friendly, tall and young.**	The receptionist is a friendly tall young woman.
20	(Listen and respond)	
21	**We live in a house that is roomy and new.**	We live in a roomy new house.
22	(Listen and respond)	
23	**We just bought a table that is old, French and interesting.**	We just bought an interesting old French table.
24	(Listen and respond)	
25	**I always wear a tie that is big, cotton and purple.**	I always wear a big purple cotton tie.

PART THREE
Grammar Drills – Student B

Unit 1 Grammar Drills Student B

You are Student B. Your partner is Student A. Your partner will start by reading a sentence. Listen and ask a question indicating surprise. Student A will check your response. Then read sentence number 2. Student A will listen and ask a question indicating surprise. Listen and check student A's response. Repeat the procedure for all statements.

Student A

Student B

I have been married nine times.

2

How many times have you been married?

What can't you ride?.

I can't ride a bicycle.

4

Who did you work with?

I worked with Bill Gates.

6

How many hamburgers have you just eaten?

I have just eaten six hamburgers.

8

Where did you study?

I studied at Harvard Business School.

10

How many children did your grandmother have?

My grandmother had ten children.

12

I weighed 12 pounds when I was born.

14

How much did you weigh when you were born?

He lives on a boat.

16

Where does he live?

I made a million dollars on the stock market.

18

How much did you make on the stock market?

I drank nine cups of coffee yesterday.

20

How many cups of coffee did you drink yesterday?

My boss plays golf every day.

22

How often does your boss play golf?

I wrote to the prime minister.

24

Who did you write to?

That painting is 450 years old.

26

How old is that painting?

Unit 2 Grammar Drills Student B

You are Student B. Your partner is Student A. Look at the mini-dialogue in number 1. Student A will read a sentence. Try to say the correct phrase to complete the dialogue. Student A will listen to your response and correct it if necessary. Then swap roles for number 2. Proceed in the same way for all the mini-dialogues.

Student A   **Student B**

1   (listen)

    _____ I was born in Tokyo.

2   I went to England last year.

So did I.   I went to London and Manchester.

3   (listen)

    _____ I want something else.

4   I've never eaten lobster before.

I have.   I eat it once a week.

5   (listen)

    _____ She says I should do it myself.

6   I've never received top marks at our university.

Neither have I.   The classes are too difficult.

7   (listen)

    _____ She didn't care about my grades.

60

8

I can swim.

So can I. I learned when I was young.

9

(listen)

_____ My mother thinks he is lazy.

10

I agree with our teacher.

So do I. I think she is absolutely right.

11

(listen)

_____ I don't need the money.

12

I never went to a concert before I moved here.

I did. I went to lots of concerts.

13

(listen)

_____ That is quite a coincidence.

14

John is moving to Russia at the end of term.

So am I. I'm going to Moscow.

15

(listen)

_____ It's too hard.

Unit 3 Grammar Drills Student B

Your partner will read out the first sentence. Listen and try to complete the sentence with the correct question tag. Your partner will check your response. Then read out the next sentence but do not read out the question tag. Your partner will try to complete the sentence with the correct question tag. Check their response against the question tag in brackets. Repeat for all 30 sentences and question tags.

1.   (Listen to your partner and add the correct question tag.)

2. **She's a doctor,**   **(isn't she?)**

3.   (Listen to your partner and add the correct question tag.)

4. **They don't live in this apartment,**   **(do they?)**

5.   (Listen to your partner and add the correct question tag.)

6. **We're going home early today,**   **(aren't we?)**

7. (Listen to your partner and add the correct question tag.)

8. **You drive a fast car,**   **(don't you?)**

9.   (Listen to your partner and add the correct question tag.)

10. **John has been studying hard,**   **(hasn't he?)**

11. (Listen to your partner and add the correct question tag.)

12. **He never washes the dishes,**   **(does he?)**

13. (Listen to your partner and add the correct question tag.)

14. You didn't marry your first girlfriend,   (did you?)

15. (Listen to your partner and add the correct question tag.)

16. She has read this book,   (hasn't she?)

17. (Listen to your partner and add the correct question tag.)

18. You're not English,   (are you?)

19. (Listen to your partner and add the correct question tag.)

20. You can't speak Spanish,   (can you?)

21. (Listen to your partner and add the correct question tag.)

22. He never says a word,   (does he?)

23. (Listen to your partner and add the correct question tag.)

24. His parents used to live in Indonesia,   (didn't they?)

25. (Listen to your partner and add the correct question tag.)

26. You're not allergic to seafood,   (are you?)

27. (Listen to your partner and add the correct question tag.)

28. This sofa is pretty comfortable,   (isn't it?)

29. (Listen to your partner and add the correct question tag.)

30. There's nothing interesting on television tonight,   (is there?)

Unit 4 Grammar Drills Student B

With your partner, take turns to convert the sentences below from active to passive or from passive to active. Your partner will read out the odd-numbered sentences for you to convert from active to passive or from passive to active. For each of the even-numbered sentences, read out the version in **bold type**. Your partner will then convert it from active to passive or from passive to active as appropriate.

	Active	Passive
1	(Listen and respond)	
2	**Every month, the group leader writes a report.**	Every month, a report is written by the group leader.
3	(Listen and respond)	
4	The students were unloading the books when I arrived.	**The books were being unloaded by the students when I arrived.**
5	(Listen and respond)	
6	**Over a million tourists have visited that attraction.**	That attraction has been visited by over a million tourists.
7	(Listen and respond)	
8	Most students had already found a permanent job before the end of the course.	**A permanent job had already been found by most students before the end of the course.**
9	(Listen and respond)	
10	**The college cinema is screening the new Magma Cloud movie.**	The new Magma Cloud movie is being screened by the college cinema.

11	(Listen and respond)	
12	When the time is up, most of the students will have completed the test.	**When the time is up, the test will have been completed by most of the students.**
13	(Listen and respond)	
14	**He said the dog had eaten his homework.**	He said his homework had been eaten by the dog.
15	(Listen and respond)	
16	Vegans can not eat this meal.	**This meal can not be eaten by vegans.**
17	(Listen and respond)	
18	**The professor helped me.**	I was helped by the professor.
19	(Listen and respond)	
20	The district manager might promote three employees.	**Three employees might be promoted by the district manager.**
21	(Listen and respond)	
21	**The Beatles wrote many famous songs.**	Many famous songs were written by the Beatles.
23	(Listen and respond)	
24	The Royal Society is going to invite a hundred guests to a gala dinner.	**A hundred guests are going to be invited to a gala dinner by the Royal Society.**
25	(Listen and respond)	
26	**A ghost scared away the visitors.**	The visitors were scared away by a ghost.

Unit 5 Grammar Drills Student B

With your partner, take turns to solve the tasks below. For each odd-numbered sentence, your partner will read out the *prompt verb* and a sentence. Repeat the sentence you hear and try to replace the word **what** with the correct participle formed from the prompt verb. Your partner will check your answer. For each even-numbered sentence, read out the *prompt verb* and the sentence that follows it. Your partner will repeat the sentence and try to replace the word **what** with the correct participle formed from the prompt verb. Check your partner's answer against the key.

1. *Excite*

2. *Surprise*   I was **what** that my son passed his test.
    Key: I was **surprised** that my son passed his test.

3. *Interest*

4. *Shock*   The news was very **what**.
    Key: The news was very **shocking**.

5. *Confuse*

6. *Disappoint*   I thought the food in that restaurant was **what**.
    Key: I thought the food in that restaurant was **disappointing**.

7. *Exhaust*

8. *Thrill*   I am **what** to meet you.
    Key: I am **thrilled** to meet you.

9. *Amaze*

10. *Depress*   He found his test results **what**.
    Key: He found his test results **depressing**.

11. *Entertain*

12. *Convince*   She didn't believe it at first, but later she was **what**.
    Key: She didn't believe it at first, but later she was **convinced**.

13. *Relax*

14. *Tire*   Working out car be very ***what***.
    Key: Working out car be very ***tiring***.

15. *Disgust*

16. *Amaze*   I am ***what*** that people can run a marathon.
    Key: I am ***amazed*** that people can run a marathon.

17. *Embarrass*

18. *Frighten*   I thought the movie was ***what***.
    Key: I thought the movie was ***frightening***.

19. *Bore*

20. *Fascinate*   My friend was ***what*** by the book.
    Key: My friend was ***fascinated*** by the book.

21. *Challenge*

22. *Confuse*   The explanation in the book was very ***what***.
    Key: The explanation in the book was very ***confusing***.

23. *Threaten*

24. *Satisfy*   She found the experience extremely ***what***.
    Key: She found the experience extremely ***satisfying***.

25. *Amuse*

26. *Annoy*   I was so ***what*** when you didn't call me back.
    Key: I was so ***annoyed*** when you didn't call me back.

27. *Worry*

28. *Relax*   A day on the beach can be very ***what***.
    Key: A day on the beach can be very ***relaxing***.

29. *Tire*

30. *Exhaust*   I was ***what*** after the marathon.
    Key: I was ***exhausted*** after the marathon.

Unit 6 Grammar Drills Student B

With your partner, take turns to solve the tasks below. For each odd-numbered sentence, your partner will read out the *prompt adjective* and a sentence. Repeat the sentence you hear and try to replace the word **what** with the correct comparative formed from the prompt adjective. Your partner will check your answer. For each even-numbered sentence, read out the *prompt adjective* and the sentence that follows it. Your partner will repeat the sentence and try to replace the word **what** with the correct comparative formed from the prompt adjective. Check your partner's answer against the key.

1. *strange*

2. *modern*   Tokyo is much **what** than Cairo.
   Key: Tokyo is much **more modern** than Cairo.

3. *comfortable*

4. *important*   Happiness is **what** than money.
   Key: Happiness is **more important** than money.

5. *safe*

6. *dirty*   New York City is much **what** than Honolulu.
   Key: New York City is much **dirtier** than Honolulu.

7. *flat*

8. *careful*   My mother is a much **what** driver than my father.
   Key: My mother is a much **more careful** driver than my father.

9. *hungry*

10. *noisy*   Diesel engines are **what** than electric motors
    Key: Diesel engines are **noisier** than electric motors.

11. *expensive*

12. *bad*   This year's financial results were **what** than last year's.
    Key: This year's financial results were **worse** than last year's.

13. *heavy*

68

14. *thin*
           The new mobile phone is a bit **what** than the previous version.
    Key: The new mobile phone is a bit **thinner** than the previous version.

15. *exotic*

16. *popular*
           Nowadays, musicals are much **what** than operatic works.
    Key: Nowadays, musicals are much **more popular** than operatic works.

17. *large*

18. *good*
           Châteauneuf du Pape is a **what** wine than Maison Latif.
    Key: Châteauneuf du Pape is a **better** wine than Maison Latif.

19. *happy*

20. *sweet*
           Oranges are much **what** than lemons.
    Key: Oranges are much **sweeter** than lemons.

21. *handsome*

22. *exciting*
           I think paragliding is a bit **what** than mountain climbing.
    Key   I think paragliding is a bit **more exciting** then mountain climbing.

23. *lucky*

24. *tall*
           I am a bit **what** than my brother.
    Key: I am a bit **taller** than my brother.

25. *afraid*

26. *long*
           The Nile is **what** than the Danube.
    Key: The Nile is **longer** than the Danube.

27. *fast*

28. *intense*
           Ultraviolet rays are much **what** than many people think.
    Key: Ultraviolet rays are much **more intense** than many people think.

29. *cool*

30. *high*
           Mount Everest is much **what** than Mont Blanc.
    Key: Mount Everest is much **higher** than Mont Blanc.

Unit 7 Grammar Drills Student B

With your partner, take turns to solve the tasks below. For each odd-numbered tasks, your partner will read out a prompt. Listen and try to form a sentence using the correct superlative form of the adjective in the prompt. Your partner will check your answer. For the even-numbered tasks, read out the prompt. Your partner will try to form a sentence using the correct superlative form of the adjective in the prompt. Check your partner's answer against the key.

	Prompt	Key
1	(Listen and respond)	
2	**Diamonds / valuable / gems**	Diamonds are the most valuable gems.
3	(Listen and respond)	
4	**The African elephant / big / land animal**	The African elephant is the biggest land animal.
5	(Listen and respond)	
6	**Egyptian cotton / soft / fabric**	Egyptian cotton is the softest fabric.
7	(Listen and respond)	
8	**The box jellyfish / dangerous / sea creature**	The box jellyfish is the most dangerous sea creature.
9	(Listen and respond)	
10	**Swimming / invigorating / exercise**	Swimming is the most invigorating exercise.
11	(Listen and respond)	
12	**The sales manager / busy / employee**	The sales manager is the busiest employee.
13	(Listen and respond)	

14	The internet / amazing / invention	The internet is the most amazing invention.
15	(Listen and respond)	
16	Mosquitos / annoying / insects	Mosquitos are the most annoying insects.
17	(Listen and respond)	
18	Louis Vuitton / exclusive / brand	Louis Vuitton is the most exclusive brand
19	(Listen and respond)	
20	The library / quiet / area	The library is the quietest area.
21	(Listen and respond)	
22	Water / healthy / drink	Water is the healthiest drink.
23	(Listen and respond)	
24	Honesty / good / policy	Honesty is the best policy.
25	(Listen and respond)	
26	Karen Mitchell / young / student	Karen Mitchell is the youngest student.
27	(Listen and respond)	
28	Dark Shadow 3 / scary / movie	Dark Shadow 3 is the scariest movie.
29	(Listen and respond)	
30	The old ford / shallow / river crossing	The old ford is the shallowest river crossing.

Unit 8 Grammar Drills Student B

With your partner, take turns to solve the tasks below. For each odd-numbered task, your partner will read out a prompt. Listen and try to reformulate the prompt using a dummy subject. Your partner will check your answer. For the even-numbered tasks, read out the prompt. Your partner will try to reformulate the prompt using a dummy subject. Check your partner's answer against the key.

	Prompt	Key
1	(Listen and respond)	
2	**Cleaning a carpet is not easy.**	It's not easy to clean a carpet.
3	(Listen and respond)	
4	**That you don't understand is obvious.**	It's obvious that you don't understand.
5	(Listen and respond)	
6	**Climbing that mountain in the winter is dangerous.**	It's dangerous to climb that mountain in the winter.
7	(Listen and respond)	
8	**That she died so young was a pity.**	It was a pity that she died so young.
9	(Listen and respond)	
10	**Will driving there take a long time?**	Will it take a long time to drive there?
11	(Listen and respond)	
12	**Living in London is great.**	It's great to live in London.
13	(Listen and respond)	

14	Reading the book twice before the exam might be a good idea.	It might be a good idea to read the book twice before the exam.
15	(Listen and respond)	
16	Learning a language is fun.	It's fun to learn a language.
17	(Listen and respond)	
18	That the store is closed on Sundays is inconvenient.	It's inconvenient that the store is closed on Sundays.
19	(Listen and respond)	
20	That he was able to finish the race was amazing.	It was amazing that he was able to finish the race.
21	(Listen and respond)	
22	Crossing the street just here seems unwise.	It seems unwise to cross the street just here.
23	(Listen and respond)	
24	Staring at a computer screen for a long time is not good for your eyes.	It's not good for your eyes to stare at a computer screen for a long time.
25	(Listen and respond)	
26	To have tried and failed is better than not to have tried at all.	It's better to have tried and failed than not to have tried at all.
27	(Listen and respond)	
28	Being on time for important meetings is always a good idea.	It's always a good idea to be on time for important meetings.
29	(Listen and respond)	
30	Listening to what she says would be better than criticising her.	It would be better to listen to what she says than to criticise her.

Unit 9 Grammar Drills Student B

Listen as your partner reads out some information. If you need to hear it again, ask your partner to repeat it. Then your partner will read out a sentence. Respond by either correcting the information or saying, 'That's right!'. Your Partner will then read out a second sentence for you to respond to in the same way. Then swap roles for number 2 and continue until all the tasks are completed.

1	(Listen and respond)	
2	Sally and Erica were sisters. Sally was born four years before Erica, but Erica was always more mature.	
2a	**Erica was more mature.**	That's right!
2b	**Erica was older.**	No, it's Sally who was older.
3	(Listen and respond)	
4	Nelson Mandela was President of South Africa from 1994 to 1999. He was the country's first black head of state.	
4a	**Nelson Mandela was President of Zimbabwe.**	No, it's South Africa that Nelson Mandela was president of.
4b	**Nelson Mandela was South Africa's first black head of state.**	That's right!
5	(Listen and respond)	
6	Hawaii and Hong Kong are both great places for a vacation. Hawaii is a tropical paradise, while Hong Kong has great night life. Both destinations are quite expensive.	
6a	**Hong Kong is an expensive place to spend a vacation.**	That's right!
6b	**Hong Kong is a tropical paradise.**	No, it's Hawaii that's a tropical paradise.
7	(Listen and respond)	

8	Golf and soccer are both popular sports in Scotland, but golf is the national game. In England, the most popular sports are soccer and cricket, but cricket is the national game.	
8a	**Soccer is the national game of Scotland.**	No, it is golf that is the national game of Scotland.
8b	**Cricket is the national game of England.**	That's right!
9	(Listen and respond)	
10	Harry Potter is a character in a series of books and movies. The first book was published in 1997. The first movie was released in 2001 and the eighth movie was released in 2011.	
10a	**The first Harry Potter book was published in 2007.**	No, it was 1997 when the first Harry Potter book was published.
10b	**The eighth Harry Potter movie came out in 2011.**	That's right!
11	(Listen and respond)	
12	When the Eiffel Tower was completed for the 1889 World Fair in Paris, it was the tallest building in the world, a record previously held by the Washington Monument.	
12a	**The Eiffel Tower was completed in 1989.**	That's right!
12b	**The 1889 World Fair was held in Washington.**	No, it's Paris where the 1889 World Fair was held.
13	(Listen and respond)	
14	The Hay Wain and Starry Night are both famous paintings. The Hay Wain was painted by John Constable in 1821. Starry Night was painted by van Gogh in 1889.	
14a	**The Hay Wain was painted by van Gogh in 1889.**	No, it's Starry Night that was painted by van Gogh.
14b	**The Hay Wain was painted by John Constable.**	That's right!

Unit 10 Grammar Drills Student B

With your partner, take turns to solve the tasks below. For each odd-numbered task, your partner will read out a prompt. Listen and try to form a sentence using the correct adjective order. Your partner will check your answer. For the even-numbered tasks, read out the prompt. Your partner will try to form a sentence using the correct adjective order. Check your partner's answer against the key.

	Prompt	Key
1	(Listen and respond)	
2	I like people who are beautiful and young.	I like beautiful young people.
3	(Listen and respond)	
4	The man bought a painting that is Japanese and large.	The man bought a large Japanese painting.
5	(Listen and respond)	
6	Our family has two poodles that are small, cute and white.	Our family has two small cute white poodles.
7	(Listen and respond)	
8	Grandma is wearing a dress that is long, black and silk.	Grandma is wearing a long black silk dress.
9	(Listen and respond)	
10	The baker made pies that were large, round and savoury.	The baker made large round savoury pies.
11	(Listen and respond)	

12	I only ate a sandwich that was tasteless and small.	I only ate a small tasteless sandwich.
13	(Listen and respond)	
14	My pet is a bird that is black and beautiful.	My pet is a beautiful black bird.
15	(Listen and respond)	
16	John is a man who is tall and thin.	John is a tall thin man.
17	(Listen and respond)	
18	They serve coffee that is delicious and Columbian.	They serve delicious Columbian coffee.
19	(Listen and respond)	
20	I have some information that is new, useful and financial.	I have some useful new financial information.
21	(Listen and respond)	
21	He gave his wife a bunch of roses that were red and fragrant.	He gave his wife a bunch of fragrant red roses.
23	(Listen and respond)	
24	This carpet is old, delightful and Persian.	This is a delightful old Persian carpet.
25	(Listen and respond)	
26	The restaurant serves curries that are delicious and Indian.	The restaurant serves delicious Indian curries.

Further classroom titles from LinguaBooks

IN A STRANGE LAND

Short Stories for Creative Learning
By Andrzej Cirocki and Alicia Peña Calvo

CEFR Level B2 - C1   ISBN 978-1-911369-18-9

IN A STRANGE LAND is an innovative and highly affordable collection of four original short stories which provide teachers with motivating and engaging classroom material at the CEFR B2 to C1 level and young adult learners with thought-provoking narratives and characters to whom they can relate.

This gripping teenage fiction encourages readers to use their imagination and interact with the texts in a variety of educational and experimental ways.

The stories are vividly illustrated and supported by creative tasks which enable students to integrate their various language skills, exploit new media, practise learning strategies and exercise autonomy.

IN A STRANGE LAND is also published as a Kindle eBook and recordings of the stories are available separately on two Audio CDs and as MP3 downloads.

LinguaBooks Adult Readers

CEFR Level C1 - C2

ELTons 2019 Innovation Awards Nominated

978-1-911369-10-3

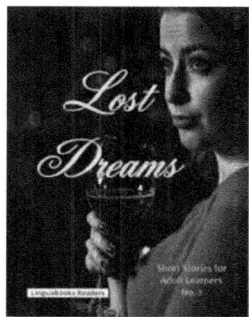

Each reader in this series consists of a collection of five original short stories with accompanying explanations, exercises and extension tasks. The focus throughout is on authenticity and originality. In this approach, the language of the stories has not been simplified for easy reading; rather, emergent difficulties are explained in the notes with further guidance provided for deeper understanding, creative extension and autonomous learning. The stories themselves present a varied mix of style and content, ranging from the surprising to the contemplative, with a touch of humour and an occasional hint of pathos.

978-1-911369-11-0

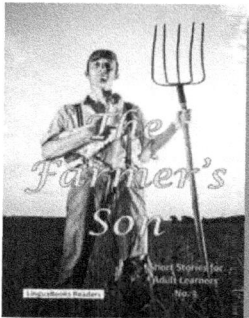

A Busker on Bow Street
Short stories for adult learners No. 1
A Busker on Bow Street / The Killer in Me / Tea for Two / The Table / Blacky

Lost Dreams
Short stories for adult learners No. 2
Lost Dreams / Annie / Almost Persuaded / Dotty / Coastal Encounter

978-1-911369-12-7

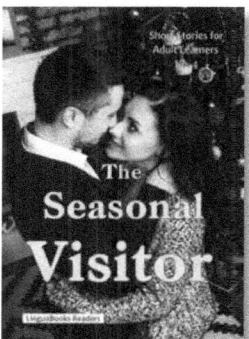

The Farmer's Son
Short stories for adult learners No. 3
The Farmer's Son / The Scarlet Dress / Ghostly Laughter / That's Cricket! / Flitzo

The Seasonal Visitor
Short stories for adult learners No. 4
The Seasonal Visitor / A Scarecrow in Winter / Land of the Dragons / The Reunion / The Fear

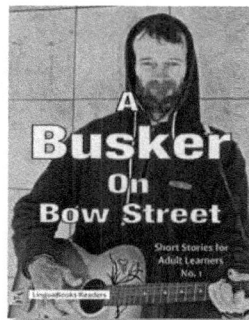

978-1-911369-13-4

Academic Presenting and Presentations

A preparation course for university students
By Peter Levrai and Averil Bolster

CEFR Level B2 - C1

This practical training course is designed to help students cultivate academic presentation skills and deal with the variety of presentation tasks they may need to master during their studies.

The material is suitable for a global audience and can be used in a wide range of academic contexts since the content not only helps learners develop their presentation skills in English but also considers wider topics relevant to English for Academic Purposes, such as principles of research and the dangers of plagiarism.

The accompanying online video presentations enable learners to immerse themselves still further in the material presented and witness first hand the impact of the techniques illustrated.

Student's Book
ISBN 978-1-911369-24-0

Teacher's Book
ISBN 978-1-911369-25-7